VISION OF THEOPHILUS

Cyril of Alexandria

Bishop of Alexandria

Translated by: Alphonse Mingana

Forward and Introduction by: D.P. Curtin

Dalcassian
Publishing
Company
PHILADELPHIA PA

Library of Congress Cataloging-in-Publication Data

Copyright © 2022 Dalcassian Publishing Co.
In association with St. Macartan Press
All rights reserved.

FORWARD

The account of the flight into Egypt does not occupy much space in the narrative of St. Matthew's Gospel. Only eleven verses record this event in the canonical narrative, and no other New Testament gospel addresses the subject or makes note of it. The act of taking refuge in Egypt is not uncommon in Jewish history: Sundry figures have sought political and economic asylum to the south in the land of Egypt, in the depths of Levantine antiquity, during the collapse of the Judahite monarchy, and from the economic pull of Ptolemaic Egypt. Moreover, the family of Christ seeking asylum in Egypt was not atypical during the Herodian period[1], and the account by St. Matthew has no shortage of known parallels[2].

However, while this text builds upon the framework of the original citation by St. Matthew, it is not wholly St. Matthew's, as the account of the Holy Family's sojourn in Egypt is considerably expanded to grant further details into their subsistence in the countryside. Perhaps the most peculiar feature of the narrative is the total absence of mention of the city of Alexandria. Notably, Alexandria was the largest Jewish city in the Roman Empire, larger even than Jerusalem, yet the family is not mentioned as approaching it. Additionally, it might be assumed that a late text produced by the Coptic church would almost certainly tie their ecclesiastical capital with that of the Holy Family. Yet, as a composition it appears largely uninterested in the relationship between the See of Alexandria and the path by which the Holy Family traveled. This grants some element of legitimacy to the folk memory of these locations, as there appears to be no secondary motive on the part of the author to promote the authority of the local bishopric.

The sites that are mentioned in the Coptic tradition appear as curiosities, as the majority of them are not major cities and would be of little interest to a 1st century Jewish family. Moreover, the sites mentioned in this narrative appear to have been centers of the early Coptic church from its foundation, rather than assigned as salient sites by this text at some later date. These sites include:

Pelusium- (*Arabic:* الفرما; *Coptic:* ⲠⲈⲣⲈⲘⲞⲨⲚ; *Greek:* Πηλουσιον) Today known as Farma, it historically has been considered the gateway to Egypt from Asia.

---

[1] France, R. T. (1981). "Scripture, Tradition and History in the Infancy Narratives of Matthew". In France, R. T.; Wenham, David (eds.). *Gospel Perspectives: Studies of History and Tradition in the Four Gospels*. Vol. 2. Sheffield (UK): JSOT Press. p. 257.
[2] Albright, W. F.; Mann, C. S. (1971). *Matthew*. Anchor Bible. Vol. 26. p. 17.

As a significant metropolis, it would have been impossible for the family to have avoided this city. As a frontier outpost on the edge of Nile civilization the Ptolemies had maintained a large fortress[3] on-site, which was the location of invasions by both the Roman Republic and the earlier Seleucid Empire.

Bubastis- (*Arabic:* الزقازيق; *Greek:* Βούβαστις; *Coptic:* ⲠⲞⲨⲂⲀⲤϮ) Today it is the modern city of Zagazig, founded there in the 19th century. The ancient city appears to have been inhabited well into the Byzantine period. The city was a major shrine to the Egyptian deity Bastet, but by this point in time was in major decline and was associated with the Hellenic deity Artemis. Bubastis was a major Christian city by the early 4th century as its bishop, Harpocration, attended the 1st Council of Nicaea.

Mostorod- (*Arabic:* علمهما; *Greek:* Μωστορod) Today known as Al-Mahamah. This place is not a town, only a stopping-off point, where, according to legend, the Christ child was bathed in the Nile River. The Holy Family was said to have passed by this way on their return to Judea. A medieval coptic church called St. Mary in Mostrod stands on the site.

Belbeis- (*Arabic:* بلبيس; *Coptic:* ⲪⲈⲖⲂⲈⲤ) Also known as the city of Phillipos, which was dedicated to the cult of the feline deity Bes, as the name of the city suggests. Belbeis was both a fortress city and one with a large Jewish population. This site is identified in connection with Leontopolis, the alleged 'land of Onias': that is to say, the land previously imparted on the ousted Jewish High Priest Onias IV by the Ptolemaic pharaohs of Egypt. Very little is known about this 'other' Jewish temple, which was shut down by Roman authorities during the First Jewish War in 70 AD. The sole Coptic tradition stemming from this site is that the Holy Family stopped here to rest. A Cathedral church stands here dedicated to Mar Gerges (St. George).

Daqadous- (*Arabic:* دقادوس; *Coptic:* ⲦⲔⲈⲢⲖⲓ) Coptic tradition makes note of a well from which the Holy Family allegedly drank. Its name, which literally means 'shrine', was almost certainly a cultic site, but to which deity is unknown.

Sebennytus- (*Arabic:* سمنود; *Coptic:* ⲬⲈⲘⲚⲞⲨϮ; *Greek:* Σεβέννυτος) Today this city is known as Samannud, which appears to be an Arabic transliteration of

---

[3] Stanley, J.-D., Bernasconi, M. P., & Jorstad, T. F. (2008). Pelusium, an Ancient Port Fortress on Egypt's Nile Delta Coast: Its Evolving Environmental Setting from Foundation to Demise. *Journal of Coastal Research*, 24(2), 451–462.

its ancient name. A temple dedicated to Anhur, god of war, was here and active in the first century. In antiquity the city was a major seat for international trade. Allegedly the Virgin Mary prepared bread here, and the local Coptic community holds in its memory a large granite baking dish said to have been used by her. A church stands on this site dedicated to the 'Virgin Mary and the martyr Abanoub in Samannoud'.

Belqas- (*Arabic:* بلقاس*; Greek:* φυλακῆς) This is a small village on the edge of the Egyptian coast. It is a strange location on two counts: Firstly, it is completed surrounded by swamp, and difficult to enter; and secondly, it appears to be a Greek garrison town, as its name means something like 'a military camp', presumably one associated with the various Greek armies utilized by Egyptian pharaohs for the five centuries prior. Alternative versions of the Holy Family's itinerary in Egypt mention a certain Alberlus or Almtala, which is perhaps the modern village of Tala.

Xois- (*Arabic:* سخا*; Greek:* Ξόις*; Coptic:* ϭⲱⲟⲩ) Also known as Sakha or Khaset, this is the village where the Christ child allegedly left a footprint on the ground which caused a well to form. In antiquity it was renowned for its wine production and trade with the rest of the Mediterranean world.

Hermopolis Minor- (*Arabic:* دمنهور*; Greek:* Ἑρμοῦπόλις μικρά*; Coptic:* ⲡϯⲙⲓⲛϩⲱⲣ) Today the minor city of Damanhur, not far from the city of Alexandria. In ancient times it was associated with the god Thoth, although by this point in antiquity its relationship was stronger to the Hellenic god Hermes, and thus its Greek name. What is curious is that the family did not proceed to Alexandria, which is the next city along this road, but went south into the treacherous deserts of western Egypt. Again, local legends associate an ancient tree with healing properties with the presence of the Holy Family.

Scentis- (*Arabic:* وادي النطرون*; Coptic:* ϣⲣⲏⲧ) Remains a major site of Coptic monasticism since the early 4th century. In the later Ptolemaic period/early Roman period it was predominantly known as a salt mine and was largely uninhabited. The local workforce was vital to the domestic industries of glass making, mortuary embalming, and Egyptian medicine. Strabo makes the first known reference to it in the 1st century BC (*Geography, 17.1*), noting the local devotion to Serapis. It appears to have been largely inhabited by foreigners during this period[4], which would explain the presence of the devotion to the Greco-Egyptian creole deity. Unlike the others, this site has no attachment to the former Ptolemaic Egyptian military.

Heliopolis- (*Arabic:* المطرية; *Coptic:* ⲱⲛ) Modern El Matareya specifically. Heliopolis proper is perhaps one of the most important cities in Egypt with its ancient priesthood extending back to prehistory. The city obtains its Greek name 'city of the sun' due to its dedication to the Egyptian deity Ra, who was worshiped here. Strabo reports that by the late Ptolemaic period Heliopolis was largely abandoned by its populace, saving only the ancient priesthood. The Holy Family is said to have abided here in the Ain Shams neighborhood. An ancient sycamore tree is venerated by locals who believe that the family rested against the tree before moving onwards.

Babylon Fortress- (*Arabic:* حصن بابليون; *Coptic:* ⲡⲁⲃⲓⲗⲱⲛ) This area today is known as the city of Fustat, which was founded in the 7th century by the armies of the Caliphate. There is an ancient church in the spot, allegedly the oldest church in the land of Egypt: Sts. Sergius and Bacchus in the Cave. The original church basilica was built in the 4th century over an older house-church. By Coptic tradition it is built over the home of the Holy Family, who resided there while Joseph worked at the local fortress. This is perhaps the folkloric origins of the Roman physician Celsus' claim that Christ was a workman in Egypt as a youth (*Origen, Against Celsus 1.28*). During the Augustan era, in which Christ lived, the fortress was a major hub of Roman military activity, being the garrison town of three Roman legions.

Maadi- (*Arabic:* معادي; *Coptic:* ⲡⲓⲙⲟⲛⲁⲥⲧⲉⲣⲓⲟⲛ ⲙ̀ⲡⲓⲟⲙⲓ) Today part of the suburbs of Cairo, its Arabic name means 'the ferries', the ancient craft of which appear to have been practiced here for the last fifty centuries.

Memphis- (*Arabic:* مَنْف ; *Greek:* Μέμφις; *Coptic:* ⲙⲉⲙϥⲓ) The ancient capital city of Egypt going back to its earliest dynasties. At its height during the pharaonic period, the Great Temple of Ptah was a major site of religious pilgrimage, and there were three other minor temples dedicated to the same deity. It appears to have been intact when Strabo (*Geographica, 17:31-31*) and Diodorus Siculus (*Bibliotheca Historica, 1.1.12,15, 24*) visited it during the late

---

[4] Mikhail, M., Moussa M. (eds), 'The Multiethnic Character of the Wadi al-Natrun', in Maged S.A. Mikhail, and Mark Moussa (eds), *Christianity and Monasticism in Wadi al-Natrun: Essays from the 2002 International Symposium of the Saint Mark Foundation and the Saint Shenouda the Archimandrite Coptic Society* (Cairo, 2009; online edn, Cairo Scholarship Online, 14 Sept. 2011),

Ptolemaic period. Memphis started its decline early in the Roman period, due to the cosmopolitan rise of Alexandria and the collapse of the various Egyptians cults which had their headquarters there. The arrival of the Holy Family in Memphis in the 1st century would have been the beginning of the city's long decline on the eventual road to oblivion. Today it is known by its Arabic transliteration 'Mit Rahina'. They allegedly sailed on from this port further down the Nile river.

Oxyrhynchus- (*Arabic:* دير الجرنوس; *Coptic:* ΠΗΙ ΙϹΟΥϹ; *Greek:* ὄργανος) The ancient names for this site vary; sometimes it is rendered as Arganus. The modern name Deir el-Garnus specifies it as a monastery. Its Koine Greek name suggests that it was originally used to determine the depth of the Niles river in antiquity. Its Coptic name is the most intriguing, as it is simply known as 'the house of Jesus'. A Byzantine church was built on the site sometime in the early 6th century with an attached well where the Christ child is said to have drunk. While it appears to be outside the Egyptian city of Osyrhynchus proper, today this district is known as Al Bahnasa.

Samalut- (*Arabic:* سمالوط; *Coptic:* ΤϹЄΜΟΥΛΟΤ) The Empress Helena visited here in the early 4th century to construct a church on the site. It does not appear to be a site of any particular importance to either Roman or Ptolemaic Egypt. If a village stood here at the time of Christ, it was largely insignificant. Today a monastery at Gebel al-Teir, or Mountain of Birds, stands commemorating the site. By Coptic tradition the family was almost killed here from a falling boulder.

Hermopolis Major- (*Arabic:* الأشمونين; *Coptic:* ШΜΟΥΝ; *Greek:* Ἑρμοῦπόλις μεγάλη) Today known as El-Ashmonein. In the late Ptolemaic and early Roman period, it was the center for the cultic worship of Thoth and Set, thus the Greek name, as Thoth was synchronized with Hermes. Hermopolis was also a major administrative capital during both periods. Pilgrimage to the site appears as early as the late 4th century, although this tradition seems to be well established at this point in history and is likely indicative of a much older tradition. It was at Hermopolis allegedly where the idols of the Egyptians smashed themselves in the presence of the Christ child, and where there were a large number of miracles performed. The tree called 'Persis' is also attested here, and found in the work of Sozomen of Constantinople, who worshiped the infant Christ as he entered the city's east gate. Sozomen's account in the 4th century makes note of the ancient temple in Hermopolis, already in ruins during his lifetime. An ancient Byzantine church remains in the former center of the city dedicated to the Holy Virgin and St. Wadamon. The Coptic Synaxarium (*Mesori 18*) mentioned an account of the latter's life and martyrdom, wherein he let the Holy family stay at his home in Hermopolis, and was later killed by its denizens. His name suggests that he was a local Egyptian, and perhaps an acolyte in the cult of Amon.

Tarot Serapamon- (*Arabic:* ديروط الشريف; *Coptic:* ⲦⲈⲢⲰⲦ ⲤⲀⲢⲀⲠⲀⲘⲰⲚ) This site is better known today by its arabic name Dayrut al-Sharif. It is a relatively small village south of Hermopolis. In the time of Christ there was very little here. However, there is an ancient Coptic monastery in the town called Abba Serapamon, wherein the town receives its Coptic name. The identity of this Serapamon is noted in the Coptic Synaxarium where he is called the 'son of Abraham, son of Levi, son of Joseph, brother to Simon" (*Hatur 28*), and of the tribe of Judah from Jerusalem. This is perplexing as this would make him a figure of the early second century, and likely a member of Christ's family through Cleophas. However, the Synaxarium further claims that he is a figure of the late 3rd century, associating him with the bishop Theonas of Alexandria. His name appears to be a cognate of the Egyptian deity Serapis and Amon, which would be more common to a convert then an observant Jew of the period. In all likelihood this is likely two separate historical individuals who have been merged together to form this folk hagiographical tradition.

Lycopolis- (*Arabic:* أسيوط; *Greek:* Λυκόπολις; *Coptic:* ⲤⲒⲞⲞⲨⲦ) Here the god Osirius was worshiped by the denizens of the city in the form of a wolf. The modern Egyptian city of Asyut is built on top of ancient Lycopolis.

Cusae- (*Arabic:* القوصية; *Coptic:* ⲔⲰⲤⲈⲒ; *Greek:* Κοῦσαι) Near the modern successor city of El Quseyya. There appears to have been a temple erected during the Ptolemaic period to Hathor/Aphrodite in the city[5], who was allegedly its patron goddess. This appears to be the primary city of interest to the text of the *Vision of Theophilus*. Its focus is strange, as it is a relatively minor city in Upper Egypt with no strong metropolitan ties to the Roman state administration or the ecclesiastical order in Alexandria. It is perhaps sufficient to note that the town was dedicated to a patron goddess, one associated with motherhood and celestial queenship[6]. Her venerable status being supplanted by the Virgin Mary in late antiquity seems like a natural transition between the decaying state of the ancient Egyptian religion and that of Coptic Christianity. It is also in Cusae that the Holy family are said to have encountered the character named Moses, who is said to be kin to Joseph the

---

[5] Llewellyn-Jones, Lloyd, and Stephanie Winder, 'The Hathoric Model of Queenship in Early Ptolemaic Egypt: The Case of Berenike's Lock', in Ian Rutherford (ed.), *Greco-Egyptian Interactions: Literature, Translation, and Culture, 500 BC–AD 300* (Oxford, 2016; online edn, Oxford Academic, 21 Apr. 2016),

[6] Lesko, B.S. (1999). *The Great Goddesses of Egypt*. University of Oklahoma Press. P. 82-23

Carpenter. This Jewish name is uncommon for the period, but still in use. However, there appears to be little to no Jewish community in this region of Egypt at the time, which leaves his appearance as being relatively mysterious.

Maqabir Meir- (Arabic: مقابر مير)- This is a relatively small village not far from the city of Cusae that was largely used as its necropolis. The city appears to have been still engaged in mortuary commerce during the 1st century. The Coptic tradition associated the citizens of Meir as welcoming the Holy family, in sharp contrast to that of Cusae.

Mount Kushkam- There remains a monastery at this site known as the Monastery of the Virgin Mary underneath which there is a cave that was used in antiquity. The monastery appears to be of the late Byzantine period, although the altar stone is dated 737 AD[7], after the Arab conquest. Today the region is called Deir el-Muharraq, or rather the 'burned monastery', citing a destruction of the site during the medieval period. Amongst modern Coptic pilgrims it is considered to be second only to Jerusalem itself. However, little information about the site, its antiquity, and the residency of the Holy family come down to us. Moreover, the reason for seeking asylum in this place is all the more puzzling, as it has no unique advantage over any major Egyptian city of the period.

Mount Dronka- Again the holy family is said to have taken refuge here in a cave near the city of Lycopolis; and again, there is little clarity to why they would have selected this site. The monastery on site appears to be quite old, perhaps from the middle of the 4th century, when monastic institutions were being founded. Moreover, it does not appear to be present in all accounts of the Holy family in Egypt. From here they returned to Judea by the route that they came following the death of Herod the Great, sometime after the year 4 BC.

While some of these sites appear to be spurious, as they are later anachronisms, or would have no way of being preserved in the local folk memory, most do appear to be reasonable for the period. Many of these are large Egyptian cities, wherein any traveler would have to pass through to navigate the local landscape. What is apparent from the legends of this sojourn is that: 1) the family spent a large amount of time in the Heliopolis area, which claims the largest number of local legends about the Christ child; and 2) the connections of these sites to the, then defunct, Ptolemaic military. The majority of the sites noted were present or former garrison towns, some of which were utilized by the novel Roman administration in the region, such

---

[7] Timm, Stefan. *Das christlich-koptische Agypten in arabischer Zeit*. p. 751.

as with the Babylon Fortress. This association between the Holy family's Egyptian itinerary and the relatively terse note by Epiphanius of Salamis, that Christ's paternal grandfather was a soldier named 'Jacob Pantera' (*Panarion 78.7.5*), would lend itself to deduce that these data points are potentially related. However, as a point of discerning historical relationships, including the ancient validity of these legends, this correlation is limited at best. What is more, with no points of clear corroboration, this remains entirely speculative.

THE TEXT OF THE VISION OF THEOPHILUS

Again, the third Book containing the flight according to the vision shown to Theophilus[8], Patriarch of the great city of Alexandria, concerning the arrival of our Lady Mary, Mother of God, in the land of Egypt, and concerning the house which she and her beloved Son Jesus Christ inhabited in the holy mountain of Ḳuskam[9], on account of their great fear of King Herod.

The reason for the journey of the Patriarch and his coming was to see great and heavenly visions, and also Theodosius the younger, the orthodox Emperor, because this Emperor gave him the keys of the temples of the idols

---

[8] This Theophilus is the historic bishop of Alexandria between 384 and 412. His episcopacy was particularly violent because of the various riots between Christians and the remaining pagans in Egypt.

[9] This site appears to be the modern 'El Quseyya'. At the time it would have been known by its Greek name 'Cusae' (Κοῦσαι), or perhaps as 'Kosei' (ⲕⲱⲥⲉⲓ) in Coptic. At the time of the composition of this text the Roman Legio II Flavia Constantia were encamped outside of the township. There appears to be an early Coptic Bishopric present here beginning in the 3rd century, but there are no earlier documents to suggest its prominence as a site of pilgrimage.

of all Egypt[10] from Alexandria to Assuan[11], in order that he might take the wealth contained in them and spend it in erecting buildings for the Church of our Lord Jesus Christ.

When he reached Assuan from the eastern side of the mountain and returned in following the western side of the mountain, there were with him ten Bishops of Upper Egypt, who spoke to him concerning the honor due to this holy house, and he expressed the desire to repair the Church that was in it in order that he might be blessed by it and obtain its benedictions. They reached the Church three days before the festival of the mother of God[12], which falls on the twenty-second of the Coptic month of Tubah, which is the sixteenth of January. The Father-Bishops and all the monks who inhabited this holy mountain[13], who were three hundred in number, besought him to remain with them till after the feast of Mary, the mother of God, and then return in the peace of our Lord. Amen!

Now, O my brethren and beloved in Christ, I shall begin to speak of what I saw and heard in this holy mountain. It is imperative to give thanks to God who kept me until I reached this holy mountain, the mountain which God chose to inhabit. And He dwelt there with His mother, the holy Virgin, as it is written: "God hath chosen Zion and hath made it His habitation." The Lord dwelt in this holy mountain and the Lord shall dwell in it. The Lord loved this holy mountain and dwelt in it with His holy and Virgin mother. He glorified it more than the towns of all the world, and He did not wish to inhabit another house, nor did He choose the house of a rich man, but He inhabited this forsaken mountain in which dwelt no man as David says: "Because the Lord was pleased with Zion and chose it as a dwelling-place," and there He dwelt.

O you holy mountain who became a dwelling-place to the Lord and a cause of joy and exultation to the angels and to all the inmates of heaven, who praise their creator who dwelt in you! Blessed are you, O holy mountain, which has been glorified more than all the mountains of heaven, and which has been exalted above the mountains of heaven, because the Lord came

---

[10] This appears to have some parallel in Byzantine sources, wherein Theophilus had the Mithraeum and Serapeum to be closed and had many of the idols taken from the temples to be publicly mocked (Socrates Scholasticus, Ecclesiastical History XVI).

[11] Perhaps better known in the Anglosphere as 'Aswan'.

[12] This is a textual error on the part of the author. The feast on the 24th of Tubah was dedicated to the departure of St. Mary the Ascetic, not belonging to the Virgin Mary according to the Coptic Synaxarium.

[13] The name of this monastery is curiously missing, which makes its identification frustrating. Since there are limited historic monasteries in Upper Egypt it may have been abandoned and forgotten in antiquity. However, alternatively, it may be the monastery of St. Pachomius which was founded in the 4th century and remains outside of Luxor.

down upon this holy mountain as He came down once upon mount Sinai, and there was joy, jubilation and dazzling light so that no one was able to go near the mountain and perceive except the prophet Moses; and no one was able to see the face of the Lord and live; but we saw Him in this holy mountain and we saw Him on the holy Throne, and we saw Him in Bethlehem when He became a man for us and put on a body from our Lady, the holy Virgin Mary, mother of God. We were sitting in darkness and in shadow of death, until He came and had mercy upon us, He who is good and lover of men, and until He repaired to these countries which were immersed in paganism more than all the world, and He illuminated us with the light of His divinity and His exalted glory.

This holy mountain resembles the Mount of Olives which our Lord and His holy disciples inhabited. And you, O holy mountain, our Lord and His mother for many days dwelt in you. The prophecy of Isaiah, the greatest of the prophets, who prophesied concerning the glory of this house in which we have assembled in this day and in this hour, has been fulfilled. When he prophesied about the coming of our Lord five hundred and sixty-seven years before it took place[14] he said: "Behold a virgin shall be with child and shall bring forth a son and they shall call His name Emmanuel which being interpreted is, God with us"; he also prophesied concerning this mountain in saying: "God hath inhabited this mountain, and benediction and grace have inhabited it. Praises and canticles are in it always and forever. Kingdoms shall cease and powers shall perish, and all the peoples shall change and pass away, and we shall sit solidly on their thrones, and our name and our memory shall not change nor pass away, except by death which hangs over men universally."[15]

And you, O holy mountain, your privileges shall be eternal by the will of God; and because of the blessings which He recited over you, all the people shall come to you, receive your blessings and ask for forgiveness for their sins, according to the saying of the prophet Isaiah: "And it shall come to pass in the latter days that the mountain of the Lord shall be established above all the mountains and shall be exalted above everything, and nations shall flow into it, and all the multitudes shall rejoice at this mountain of the God of Jacob; and He will make the path straight for us in order that we may walk in it, for out of Zion shall go forth the law, and the words of the Lord from

---

14 This is perhaps a strange period of time being citing. Assuming that they had not made the error attributed to Dionysius Exiguus, this would place Isaiah in 573 BC, nearly a century and a half from his ascribed lifetime.
15 This is not a quote from Isaiah but does loosely appear to be similar to that of Daniel 2:44. This would also make more sense considering the previous timeline being noted of some five centuries passing, rather than the seven for it to be Isaiah.

Jerusalem."[16] You are truly the mountain of the Lord, and the house of the God of Jacob, because the one who established the law has dwelt in you with His mother, the holy Virgin Mary; and the way to this place is by faith, and everyone walks to-day to this derelict mountain, from towns and villages, and narrates the glory of this holy and pure house. Truly this is the desert of life, this is the stretch of land chosen by the holy Virgin, our Lady Mary, and her Son, our Lord Jesus Christ.

St. John the Evangelist[17], the son of Zebedee and the beloved of our Lord, testified in the Apocalypse and said: "I saw a woman clothed with the sun, and the moon under her feet, and upon her head a crown of twelve stars. And I saw a serpent standing before her expecting her child that he might kill him, a child who rules the world with a rod of iron, and who went up to heaven to God, and unto His holy throne."[18] And John said also: "I saw a dragon casting water out of his mouth after the woman that he might drown her in water. And the earth welcomed the woman, was rent and swallowed the water which the serpent had cast out of his mouth after her. And there were given unto the woman wings of a bird, and she flew to the mountains, to a place prepared to her by God, and she inhabited it one thousand two hundred and three-score days, which makes three years, five months and ten days. And the serpent waxed wroth with the woman and went away to her children to sow the seed of war between him and them. And they kept the commandment of our Lord and the orders of Jesus."

The woman whom we have mentioned above is Mary, the mother of Jesus. She is truly the Queen of all women. The sun in which she is arrayed is our Lord and Savior Jesus Christ, who dwelt in her and illuminated all her body, and the moon is John the Baptist who was illuminated by the baptism of Christ, with which we clothed ourselves for the forgiveness of sins. And the crown of twelve stars over her head are our Fathers, the holy Apostles, through whom mankind entered into the path of truth. And the serpent is Satan, and the water which he cast our of his mouth is the anger which went out of Herod against the children whom he slew on the occasion of the birth of our Lord Jesus Christ, whom anyone who acknowledges will fight against the same Satan for ever and ever. This wilderness in which our Lord dwelt with His mother had been prepared for them by God.

And I will say with Jacob, the father of the tribes: "This is the house of God and the meeting-place of all the saints." As the name of the Lord God liveth,

---

[16] See Isaiah 2:2-5

[17] The author here makes the common mistake in the patristic period of confabulating St. John the Apostle with St. John the Evangelist with St. John of Patmos.

[18] See Rev. 12:1

when I entered to-day into this house my soul was filled with joy, gladness and satisfaction; and I forgot all my fatigue and the length of the journey which I had to endure and the exhaustion which had overtaken me; and the cares of all the world left me because she who is our Lady, mother of Light, implored her Son and her beloved, to the effect that all who would enter into this house and pray in it shall be free from all the stratagems of Satan and the anxieties of this world.

What shall I say and what shall I utter to praise you, O our Lord Jesus Christ for the honor You did to me, me the wretched and the sinner Theophilus! You gave me your holy body and your innocent blood which I distribute to Your people for the forgiveness of their sins. You gave me a throne on which to sit while I am not worthy of it, and You elected me to shepherd Your people. You gave me a happy time, and fear forsook me; and You shut the mouth of the dragons who disturbed the peace of Your people, the dragons that are the community of the impure Heretics[19]. You gave us praiseworthy Emperors, like Theodosius the Younger, who love Your truth and enjoin it on the churches of Christ, and the fear of Arius and all his soldiers ceased; that Arius on account of whom the holy Apostle, my father Athanasius[20], suffered persecution to the extent of going from place to place for twenty-seven years, while the Emperor was seeking him on account of the lies of the wicked Heretics. God willed this in order that in suffering the persecution of the Apostles he might have their reward in the Kingdom of our Lord Jesus Christ. It was a barbarous people[21] which he was appointed to shepherd until our Lord Jesus Christ revealed Himself to it after the persecution of Father Athanasius.

And Athanasius repaired to the great city of Rome where he became worthy of the benediction of the bodies of the holy and sweet-tongued Apostles Peter and Paul, and where he saw their faces suffused with joy, and where they spoke to him real words. After this he desired to build a church under the name of John the Baptist, but he did not succeed, because he was unable to erect anything from fear of the Heretics. It happened to him what happened to the prophet David at the time when he wished to build a temple to the Lord, and he was not able to do so because of the fear and the vicissitudes that befell him. And when the Lord wished to comfort him, he said to him: "Thou shalt not do this, but the one who comes after thee shall

---

[19] He is apparently alluding to either the Origenists, who had had previously supported at the Catechetical School of Alexandria, or perhaps the remaining Arians and their supporters in the imperial court.

[20] The former bishop of Alexandria, who was frequently exiled and removed from office with the changing winds of imperial administrations.

[21] Athanasius was exiled to Gallia by the 1st Synod of Tyre.

build a house for me."[22] This happened to me, because after the death of my Father Athanasius his throne was occupied by my Father Peter[23], and when he also died he was succeeded by my Father Demetrius[24], whose office I assumed after him—the throne of the one of whom I am not worthy.

When I was ready according to the will of God, I built a church under the name of John the Baptist[25]. When I had finished it, I placed in it all the vessels of the Church. I then erected, at the back of it, a church to the Three Children[26], and in it I placed also all its vessels, while their bodies were in Babylon. We were full of joy and gladness, and the three saints appeared in the church on the day of its consecration[27], and all the congregation saw them. All this happened through the intercession of the saints according to the will of God.

And the God-loving Emperor Theodosius came to Alexandria, the city of the Christians. When the Christ-loving and believing Emperor reached the city, I, Theophilus went out to meet him with banners of crosses, accompanied by my suite and the notables of the city. We knelt before him and said to him: "Hail, O believing Emperor, O lover of Christ and of His holy cross, like the emperor Constantine in his time! Hail, O you who truly honor Christ! Hail, O you who love Christ with all your heart, you whom Christ loved and on whom He bestowed peace and majesty! You opened the doors of the Church, and the faithful had joy and honor in your time. May God open before you the door of His grace, and may He make your enemies your footstool! May the Lord who weaved a crown for you in this world, weave a crown for you with the saints in His heaven!"

And the Emperor answered and said to me several times in humility: "Hail, O saint. These things have been granted to us by God through your prayers." And "You uphold me in the righteousness of your words[28]," as David said.

We led then the emperor and brought him to the holy church of Mark the Evangelist. After he had taken the benediction of the saint, the owner of the

---

[22] See 1 Ki. 8:19
[23] Peter I, bishop of Alexandria 373-381, who sought refuge in Rome with Athanasius in the past.
[24] The list of Coptic bishops has Timotheos succeeding Peter I, who this Demetrius is is unknown. He may have been the Dean of the Catechetical School of Alexandria.
[25] This is the ancient church near the Kuskam Coptic monastery, the ruins of which are still visible to this day. It was allegedly constructed by black African monks, or perhaps Bejas.
[26] That is Shadrach, Meshach, and Abednego, the young men from the Book of Daniel, a common motif in early Christian art.
[27] That is to say the Coptic month of the 10th of Bashons
[28] See Ps.119:116

church, we led him again and proceeded to the churches which had been renovated in our time[29]. He was very pleased with them and said to me in smiling: "Blessed be the compassionate Lord God who does good things to His elect and beloved ones, and 'exalts them that are of low degree,' as the Book says: 'I shall praise those who praise me.' You, O my Father, resemble our Father Abraham who received God with His angels because of his faith, and this was counted unto him for righteousness, for ever and ever. You, O my Lord and my brother, became a friend to God and to His angels, and this is the reason why God exalted you and honored you more than the Fathers, your Fathers I mean who held the same office before you. I give you, therefore, for all time, the keys of the temples from the land of Alexandria to that of Assuan, in order that you may take from them any wealth which you will find in them and spend it in the erection of churches and monasteries, in the duration of my reign." In that very moment he ordered the keys to be given to me. Then the inhabitants of the city led him away in great honor on account of the fatigue of the journey.

Three days after this the emperor summoned me, and I went to him and stood before him. We then went out, and I walked with him, along with the notables of the city and all the priests, until we reached the temple of the Camp of Alexander in which the Great Macedonian Conqueror had stored treasures, and the door of which he had locked and sealed[30]. We found the door sealed with three seals so that no one would be able to open it. Indeed, it had never been opened from the day of Alexander down to this day in which God who opened the eyes of the blind from their mothers' womb opened it. And God opened the eyes of my mind, and I saw on the three doors three thetas–letters of the alphabet–inscribed on them. These three letters referred the first to Theos which means God, the second to Theodosius, the believing Emperor, and the third to my name Theophilus. I did not know this with my own earthly knowledge nor by my own power, but by the power of God who opened the eyes of the heart of the divine Theophilus.

In that hour the door, at the inner side of which was the great wealth, was thrown open, and the emperor saw it and was amazed at the quantity of it. They rejoiced and glorified our Lord Jesus Christ, our powerful God. And the Emperor said: "It is God that has granted us this favor and the gift of this wealth." In that very hour he gave a portion of it to the inmates of the prison, to the churches and monasteries, and to the poor, the orphans and the widows, and no one was left in want in those days, because he satisfied the

---

[29] This renovation likely took place earlier in the century.
[30] Presumably he means the Mortuary Temple of the Tomb of Alexander the Great, sealed permanently by the Emperor Septimus Severus in the 3rd century.

wants of all. He ordered what was left to be carried on a ship as far as the Capital[31]. Afterwards I walked with him along with my suite, and we said to him: "Go in the peace of the Lord, and may His help be with you! May He make your enemies your footstool and grant you happy times! May the years of your life be without fear, anxiety, and apprehension!"

And he answered and said to me: "May God be with you, O my holy Father! For God's sake do not deprive me of you prayers and supplications that are accepted by God whom you serve. May He deliver you and me in the day of trial from the demons and from the wicked wars the waves of which are rising against us like the waves of the sea! May He also give us His grace in the day of our passing away to Him, because it is He who possesses grace and grants forgiveness of sins now, always, and for ever and ever. Amen!"

When he had boarded the ship that was bound for the City of Constantinople, we returned to the city of Alexandria in great joy and praised God for having given us in our days a good and just Emperor. A few days later we wished to accomplish what was ordered by the emperor, and we went up to Egypt by the will of God, and we went round all the temples of idols, and discovered in them a considerable quantity of wealth. I distributed all this wealth to the poor and the needy, and to all the churches and monasteries on the holy mountain. I gave orders concerning the churches that were to be built, and they were erected according to my instructions.

After all this I returned by the will of God to this holy, honorable and pure mountain, and informed myself concerning the honor due to it. I was accompanied by some Father-Bishops, and I wished to go to it and be blessed by it before returning to my town. In this way I attained what was in my mind, namely, to be worthy of praying in this holy house which was the dwelling-place of God, of His angels and of His holy Virgin mother. O you holy house which resembles the heavenly Jerusalem! As God liveth, I was astonished at this desolate house more than all the corners of the earth, because it was worthy of the fact that the Son of God and His mother lived in it and did not wish to abandon this place which He had chosen in conjunction with His good Father and the Holy Spirit, to whom be glory for ever and ever. Amen!

O my brethren and my beloved, lo I have truthfully narrated to you what happened to me and to the good Emperor Theodosius the divine, me your

---

[31] This episode is strange as St. John Chrysostom says that the tomb of Alexander was unknown at the time. Other references to the tomb note that it had previously been raided by the Roman Emperors Caligula and Caracalla. This account is the only reference to the tomb in late antiquity before being noted by John of Antioch in the Byzantine period.

Father Theophilus; and also, what took place till, by the will of God, I reached this place. After this, listen O my brethren, to what I am going to say to you in good faith and in the fear of God, i.e. to the vision which the holy Virgin Mary, the mother of God, revealed for your sake, the knowledge of which I shall now impart to you:

It happened that after we had finished our nocturns and my brother-Bishops had slept in a place by themselves, I went up to the upper chamber in which the mother of God had sat in the days which she had spent in this mountain. When I rose to pray, I stretched my hands, prayed and implored God and my Savior Jesus Christ and said: "Hear me as you heard my Father Alexander till, he upheld the orthodox faith; hear me as you heard my Father Athanasius the holy Apostle, whom you helped in all his trials. Hear me in this way, who am unworthy of your service, because I am a sinner. I know that you hear me always, because you are near to all those who love your holy and pure name.

"O my Lord and my God, have mercy upon me, and do not let me return empty-handed, me who have fixed my mind on you from my childhood to my old age. I beseech you to reveal to me you're coming into the world and to this mountain which you visited together with your holy Virgin mother, and to this desolate house in which you established your habitation. I pray you to help me to build a big church, and we will glorify, exalt and honor your holy name. You are the one to whom are due power and glory with your Father and your Holy Spirit, now at all times and forever. Amen."

When my prayer was finished, a light shone on me, which was so dazzling that I believed that the sun itself was shining on me. And a throne of light appeared to me, on which was sitting the Queen of all women, the holy Virgin, our Lady Mary, Mother of God. Her face was illuminated like the sun from the light with which she was invested, and she was covered with a majestic brightness, and with her were many myriads of angels. I was so bewildered that I said: "Is there in all the world one who is able to contemplate this great majesty?" I saw Gabriel and Michael, and a great multitude of other angels with them. When I looked and saw them, I fell on my face to the ground and became like a dead man, and Michael raised me and removed fear and dread from me.

And the holy Virgin Mary, Mother of God, spoke and said to me: "Arise and fear not, O Theophilus, our servant and the athlete who fights for the Christians. Hail, O Theophilus! Arise, be strengthened, look and see that I am the mother of Jesus Christ, the Lord of heaven and earth, the mother of the one whom neither heaven nor earth are able to comprehend, the one who was nine months in my womb by His Will. I am His mother, and I gave milk from my breast to the one who feeds the world by His will. I am Mary, the daughter of Yonakhir[32], and my mother is Hannah of the tribe of Judah and of the house of David[33]. I have revealed myself to you by the will of my beloved Son: I shall show you the One who was with me, who grasped at my knees and looked at my face as all other children do when they weep before their mothers until they are carried by them.

At that moment I was carrying Him under my armpit, holding Him and kissing Him, while I was happy at my being able to walk with Him. I was cursing Herod and all his kingdom for the wickedness which he perpetrated against those holy and innocent children whom he killed and the hearts of whose parents he filled with great pain and grief. And my cousin Salome used to take my Son at all times, caress Him and smile at Him; and the blessed old Joseph used to carry the clothes in which my Son was clad and what was necessary for our food. Any time my father Joseph saw me handing the child to Salome[34], he would take Him from me to carry Him on his shoulders and play with Him.

O Theophilus, I endured great hardship before reaching this land of Egypt. While we were in the east side of the town we sat under a tree because it was the time of the first Summer, which falls on the twenty-sixth day of the month of May. Joseph fell asleep from the exhaustion of the journey; likewise, Salome slept; and I was left under the tree feeding from my breasts my Son on whom was a garment of the color of a grape[35], a color similar to that of the garment with which my parents clothed me in the Temple. After I wore that garment, I never put it off again, nor did I put off the veil which I am wearing. And the color of the sandals of my Son resembled the color of gold and silver on His feet.

When we were journeying, we met two brigands, one of whom was an Egyptian from Egypt and the other a Syrian from Syria and also a Hebrew from our land[36]. And the Syrian brigand said to the Egyptian brigand: "I should have liked to plunder the garments that are on this woman and her son, because they resemble the garments of Kings, and if I had encountered

---

[32] Elsewhere transliterated of 'Joachim', which is perhaps more familiar.

[33] It is unclear if this is intended to mean that they both are from the tribe of David, or only Hannah is of royal descent.

[34] This Salome appears to frequently in literature regarding Christ's nativity. She is either a daughter of Joseph from his previous marriage, or a mid-wife that is employed by the family.

[35] This connotates royalty in the Near East, although it would be doubtful that Mary would have worn this historically, as she was not a member of the Hasmonean dynasty, then ruling Judea. The author does appear to be familiar with the text of the Protoevangelium of James from this passage, citing Mary's residence in the Jerusalem Temple in childhood.

[36] Presumably the Syrian is also the same person as the Hebrew being mentioned here.

them in a place other than this, I would have taken those garments from them, but I have no opportunity of doing it now because they are near the town." And the Egyptian brigand said to him: "Let us proceed on our way. I never saw a child like this since I was born." And they went their way while uttering such words and conversing on this theme. Then my Son relinquished my breast that was in His mouth and asked for water and said to me: "I am thirsty, give me a little water." And I looked round me and did not find the water that my beloved Son was asking for. Then I arose, took my beloved Son and brought Him to the town and asked the women I met there for water to give Him, but none of them wished to give us anything, as the inhabitants of that town had very little compassion.

When the brigands saw me entering the town[37], they came back and went to my father Joseph; and while he was asleep, they abducted the sandals of my Son and fled. When I returned, I awakened them and said to them: "Arise and let us leave this town. I never saw people with less faith and compassion than its inhabitants, because I asked water from them and no one gave me any. The only gain that accrued to me from this town is that the sandals of my Son have been stolen!" And I wept and was distressed.

When my beloved Son noticed that I was weeping, He wiped off my tears with His holy hands, and stretched His small finger and made the sign of the cross on the earth, and instantly a spring of water was opened in it, from which water jetted forth and flowed on the ground. And we drank water as sweet as honey and as white as snow. Then my Son made the sign of the cross on the water and said: "Let this water help, make whole and heal the souls and bodies of those who shall drink of it, with the exception of the inhabitants of this town of whom none shall be healed by it."

Then we ate a little food, and I lifted my beloved Son on my arms, and we set off on our journey. In that hour the temples of the idols which were in the town fell and were smashed to pieces, and likewise the idols fell one upon another and were smashed.

And we repaired to the land of Egypt, and the mountains, the animals and the stones honored my Son, and when we walked, they walked with us. And my Son turned to those mountains, stones and animals and spoke; and He laid His right hand on the eastern mountain and His left hand on the northern mountain and said: "Stop"; and they stopped. And the traces of His two hands were impressed and are seen in the mountains as if in dough and in wax, and lo they are seen down to this day. And He said to them: "Be as a

---

[37] This story is reported in a similar manner in other literature (Arabic Gospel of the Infancy of the Savior, 10; The Gospel of Pseudo-Matthew, XXIV).

sign and a mark to all who are weak in faith concerning my coming and do not believe that I came into the world; but let the accursed unbelieving Jews and Herod be anathemas, together with those who do not believe in my holy name."

And He said to the Mountains: "You have acknowledged me and believed in me while you have neither soul nor body, and those who have a soul, and a body did not believe in me. And the kings whom I created in my likeness and in my image did not believe in me, did not receive me nor did they honor me, but endeavored to kill me till I reached this place. After this let my name and the name of my holy mother remain in power and honor for ever and ever from generation to generation."

We reached afterwards a town called Eshmunain[38]. When we approached the first gate through which we wished to enter the town, we found images of horses on all the four corners of the gate, looking towards the town. In that very hour they fell and were broken up. My beloved Son spoke to them and said to them: "You shall be a sign to this town and to its inhabitants forever and ever." And in that hour, they became as He said.

Further, there was in that place a tree which worshiped below the traces of the steps of my Son, and cried saying: "Blessed be your coming, O Lord Jesus Christ, the true Son of God." And my beloved Son spoke to it and said: "Let no worm be found in you forever but be you a remembrance to all of my entry to-day into this town." And He touched it. It is the tree called Mukanṭah[39], and it shall stand for ever. From it we entered the market of the town of Eshmunain and we saw that all its adults and children were amazed at my beloved Son and admired the glory which was dwelling in Him, and they spoke and said: "We have never met with another child like this."

After this, while we were still in the town, five camels came near us and began to walk in the market; they rendered the road too narrow for us, and my Son looked at them, and in that hour they became stones down to this day. Afterwards a believing man in whom was found the grace of God received us in his house. And all the idols which were in that town fell and were broken

---

[38] This Coptic named city (ϢΜΟΥΝ) is perhaps better known by its Ptolemaic name 'Hermopolis Magna' (Ἑρμούπολις), also known as 'Hermopolis of Upper Egypt'. The modern city of Eshmunain is a short distance away from this site. This was an extremely important Egyptian city, although it is impossible for it to be the city by which they entered Egypt, as it is a substantial distance from the Judean border. It did have a strong associated with Egyptian cultic education, as it was the site of a Temple to Thoth. An early Coptic Basilica was built on this site perhaps as early as the 4th century.

[39] The Byzantine historian Sozomen (Hist. Eccl. V, 21) calls this tree Persea. The name of the tree is likely Coptic, but its meaning is unknown.

up, and all the priests of the idols took fright and hid in their houses in a secluded place. In the morning all the people assembled in the place in which we were, and lo with them were great multitudes of persons who were sick and stricken with different diseases, and also all those who were deaf and dumb and all those who were suffering from any kind of pain. My beloved Son laid His hand on each one of them and healed them from their complaints. In that town were seen many miracles and wonders, and if I were to reveal to you all that happened there a book could not contain it.

After this a great throng of people crowded on us, and they pushed their way to me on account of the great number of miracles which my Son performed in that day. We left the town from its northern part, and we walked a short while and reached a locality called Ķenīs[40]. The inhabitants of this town were very charitable, and I remained with them several days in the place in which we first went. My blessing be on that place in the name of my Son and in my own till the last day! And my Son wrought innumerable miracles in that place, and all those who had diseases or afflictions came to Him with faith, and He healed them in His abundant grace.

After this a carpenter heard of the numerous miracles which my Son was performing, and he knew Joseph before that day, because he had come to Jerusalem and Joseph had given him hospitality. When he saw us he received us and took us to his house. He had a son who was possessed with devils from his birth, and he had in him a powerful, pitiless, and cruel demon. And when we entered that town, the demon took the boy and dashed him to the ground, and shouted from him: "What have I to do with you, O Jesus of Nazareth? Have you come to torment us before the time? We left Jerusalem to you and fled and came to this town and you followed us here in order to torment us! Verily you are the Son of God!" When he had uttered this my beloved Son said to him: "O accursed demon, shut up your mouth and come out of him." And the child was healed in that very hour. And his father and mother arose and worshiped us and said: "Blessed are we that we were found worthy of this gift more than all the world, because you entered our house while we were sinners." And they received us in their house and gave us great hospitality. And when we entered their house, the benediction of the Lord entered into them. And many people of those localities, seeing the miracles which my Son wrought believed in Him.

---

[40] This is also transliterated as Nikyas, and is associated with the modern site of Dairut al-Sharif. It is about two days south of the site of Hermopolis. This appears to have been a significant monastic site as well, as popularized the desert father Abba Sarapamon. This survives in the Coptic name of the town: Terot Serapamon (ⲧⲉⲣⲱⲧ ⲥⲁⲣⲁⲡⲁⲙⲱⲛ)

After this, notables of the town asked the priests of the idols and said to them: "Why did you not come to the temples? Why were you not seen in the town, and why did you not leave your houses?" And they answered and said: "From the day that woman who has with her a child entered the town, the idols were broken up and their temples fell. When we do our best for them in the night, we find them broken up and smashed to pieces in the morning." And they sent for us requesting us to go to them. When the messengers arrived, they found us in an upper room of the house. Then they seized the man who had invited us to his house and conducted him to the notables of the town, who said to him: "Where are those travelers who halted in your house?" And he answered and said to them: "They left my house three days ago, and I do not know where they went." And they tormented him greatly, but he did not tell them more than "I do not know where they went."

When the owner of the house came to us and informed us of what had happened to him from the chiefs and the priest, we rose up in the morning and left them and went up to the land of Egypt and reached a town called Ḳusḳam in which there was a temple of idols surmounted by an idol on which there were seven veils[41]. The priests of the temple performed the service and did not allow any man to worship there apart from the chiefs of the town; and after these had worshiped, they would present to the idols the necessary offerings.

When we reached the gate of the town the seven veils were torn asunder, and the idol fell to the ground and was smashed to pieces. And the demons who were in the idols cried out and said to the priests: "If you do not pursue that woman and the child who is with her, and the old man who is with them and the other woman, and drive them away, and if you let them enter this town, they will put an end to your service, and we will leave the town. Lo, we have informed you before they enter the town." And they scoured the other towns of the land of Egypt and said to their inhabitants: "If this woman enters your town all the temples that are in it will fall, the religion of the town will cease, our enemies will rise against us, our town will perish and all this great honor which you see will pass away. Lo, we have informed you of this before it happens." After the idols had said this, they became quiet.

When the priests of the idols, who were a hundred in number, heard the speech of the idols, they pursued us with rods and axes in order to strike at us. They bore evil faces and shouted after us and said: "Where are you going, and what is it you want from us, and what is your aim? Lo, our gods have

---

[41] There was, allegedly, a temple to the Greek goddess Aphrodite Urania, represented by a cow. The account gives no mention of the idols present, but the presence of this goddess does serve to suggest the strong Hellenic presence in this nome capital.

informed us of the way you have damaged them. Go out of this town lest the children should come out and kill you, since you wish to enter the town in order to destroy it." And they uttered to us these and similar words, while they, their women and children and their adults, chased us away.

And I carried my Son on my breast and walked away weeping. My heart was heavy and in pain and trouble because they did not receive us nor did they want us to stay with them but insulted us and drove us away. When we went a little distance from their town, my beloved Son turned and cursed the town which is called Ḳuskam, which is situated on the east side of the northern mountain of the country of Eshmunain and said thus: "Let its people be in an estate lower than that of all other people and let them be more lowly and subdued than all the inhabitants of the land of Egypt. Let its earth be cursed so that nothing shall grow in it except alfa and rush-nut, and let its soil lie uncultivated and remain as it was before I cursed it. Let its chiefs not multiply, but let them succeed one another, one at a time. Let it be lowlier than all the land of Egypt, and let the blessing of my holy virgin mother not fall on the inhabitants of the town."

After He said this and cursed the town and its inhabitants, we proceeded a short distance south of the town, and sat in a place there on account of the weariness and fatigue of the journey and partook of a little food. Now there was in the hand of the old Joseph a staff of olivewood, and my beloved Son seized it with His blessed and holy hand and planted it in that place and said: "Let it be as a benediction of the Lord in this place for ever, and a perpetual memorial of my coming to this place." And it grew up in that hour and gave fruits of olive-trees.

And we wished to proceed on our journey. There were many villages round that place, and Joseph used to stretch his finger and point them out to us, and say: "To which of these villages shall we go and halt? The day has ended, and the night has come." And I said to him: "O my father, I have no intention of going to any of these villages but take us to this mountain until we see what to do." When I said this, he walked before us and we went up to the mountain, and it was the time of the setting of the sun.

When we had a short distance left to reach our destination, lo the two brigands whom we had met before our arrival at Basṭah[42] came to us. They had followed us from place to place, and when they saw us in this deserted

---

[42] Here the previously unnamed town is mentioned, and it can be identified with the site of Tell al-Bastah. The historian Abu al-Makarim states that the family resides on the second story of the surviving mud-brick structure here.

and dry mountain they approached us with drawn weapons, hidden faces, and unsheathed swords, and said: "You have exhausted us from fatigue, because we have pursued you for many days and have not found you and have had no opportunity of meeting with you in order to plunder you, except this moment in which you have fallen into our hands. To-day we will strip you of your garments and plunder you." And they dared to lay hands on my beloved Son and snatched Him from my hand and stripped Him of the garment which He was wearing. Then they took my garments also: they even took the veil that was over my head. Afterwards they dared to lay hands on my father Joseph and stripped him of his garments while he was standing speechless like a lamb. As to Salome, when she noticed what was taking place, she threw her garments to them before they came to her.

When they took our garments they went a short distance away from us, and they began to talk to each other. When I saw them standing and taking counsel, I was greatly alarmed and said to myself: "They will perchance come and kill my Son." And I took Him on my hands, laid my face on His face, wept and said: "O my beloved Son, Oh that I were in Bethlehem! Woe is me, O my beloved Son, where shall I go in this place and where shall I flee? I fled with you from Jerusalem fearing that Herod might kill you, but O my Son, O beloved of my soul, would to God I had remained in my village and had not undergone all this fatigue in vain! I fear lest people more wicked than Herod should take you from me! Would that I were in Bethlehem, because they might have recognized the old Joseph who would have implored them not to kill you! Woe is me, O my beloved Son, because I am a virgin girl, and I do not know anything about all this.

"O light of my eyes, whom do I know in this foreign land and in this desert place? I know no village nor town. Where are those who know me, let them come and weep with me to-day! O my beloved Son, let all the women who bore sons come and see my affliction, the anxieties of my heart, and what befell me to-day! O my Son, I fled with you from place to place and endured fatigue, but I was rejoicing that no harm had come to you; these wicked brigands, however, were pursuing me and scouring countries and towns to find me. What shall I do, O my beloved Son, if I see them wishing to kill you in this place? Would that they would kill me before killing you in order that I may not see your great affliction! If they were to kill you here, I would kill myself with my own hands, O my beloved Son! O my beloved Son, how much shall I miss the sweet words you spoke to me every day! What shall I do, O light of my eyes and health of my limbs!

"Woe shall come on me, when I see other women feeding their children from their breasts. I shall seek those women whose children have been killed by the cruel Herod in order that they may come and weep with me to-day. Would that I were in Jerusalem or in Bethlehem, because there I could have found many women to come and wail with me! I implore to-day my holy fathers and the prophets to weep with me! I implore the angel Gabriel who announced to me your conception and your birth to look at my lamentation over you! And would that I were also with Elizabeth my kinswoman and her son John, so that they might see my affliction! O my Lord, have mercy upon me and upon my exile, and do not neglect my supplication and affliction!"

While I was uttering such words and lamenting and weeping, my tears came down my cheeks, and to the cheeks of my Son. One of the brigands looked and saw me weeping, and his nerves shook, and he spoke with his companion who was a Jew and said to him: "O my companion, I beseech you to-day not to take the garments of these strangers, because I notice on their faces a light greater than that of all the faces of mankind. This child resembles a Prince the like of whom I have never seen."

And the Jewish brigand said to the Egyptian brigand, his companion: "I will not listen to you this time as I wish to take their garments because they are royal garments which will bring us much wealth for our living." When he noticed that he was determined to do his wicked will and take the garments, he said to him: "O my brother, we shall steal in the coming night, and you will take the two portions, mine and yours. Last night we also had a good haul, and you know that I had a good part of it. Let all this be yours but give me the garments of these strangers as my portion, and I will return them to their owners, because their nakedness has much disturbed me, especially that of this Child." And the Jewish brigand said to him: "Take them as part of your portion." And the Egyptian brigand took them as part of his portion and gave them back to us.

When we wore our garments and put the garments of my beloved Son on Him, He looked at the brigand and stretched His finger and made the sign of the cross on Him. And the two brigands proceeded on their way. And my beloved Son turned and said to me: "O Mary, my holy and virgin mother, the Jews will crucify with me in Jerusalem these two brigands whom you see, and one of them will be on my right hand and the other on my left. The Egyptian will be crucified on my right hand, and the Jew on my left, and the brigand who returned our garments will confess me and believe in me on the Cross and will first enter Paradise before Adam and all his other children. You see also this spot where they have stripped me of my garments and you have shed your sweet tears over my body: all the sick persons who shall come to it in future and who shall be stripped on it of their garments and be bathed in it, I shall heal them as an honor and commemoration of the fact that I had been stripped there of my garments, and your tears had fallen on my body. They will be made whole, and they will return home with joy and gladness."

When He said this the night became slightly darker, and the blessed old Joseph quarreled with me and said to me: "I told you that we ought to go to one of these villages before the night came, and you did not listen to me; now we have reached this desert place, and the night came, and I do not know where to go. If God had not kept us by His grace we would have been killed by these brigands." And my beloved Son smiled in the face of Joseph and said to him: "O father, do not speak harshly to my holy virgin mother. It is the will of my good Father that I should perform all things dealing with humanity. It is not you who direct me, it is I who direct all the world and conduct you wherever I wish."

After He said this we came up to this mountain and to this forsaken house into which we entered. I stood in the middle of it and put down my Son from my breast, and it was very dark. When my Son stood on His holy feet on the ground, He stretched His hands and they emitted beams of light like the sun when it rises, and we thanked God and expressed gratitude to Him for the fact that He had helped us to reach this place, safe from unjust men. We spent the night in the house in great joy and blessed God all the night.

At daybreak we discovered a well of water to bathe my Son, and also for drinking. We were so pleased that we had found water! When I carried my Son and brought Him to the well, He stretched His finger and blessed it, and it became full, and water surged up immediately to its mouth. And He opened His holy mouth and blessed the water saying: "Let it be sweet in the mouth of everyone, like the water of the river is to the inhabitants of Egypt, and let it heal all those who bathe in it in true faith."

When we went into the house we sat down, I, my Son, Joseph and Salome. And Salome walked about and found a wash-basin and a water-jug as if they had been placed there for us. It was Salome who always bathed my Son, and I gave milk to Him while He was feeding all the world; but our food used to come from God. On many occasions while I was quiet and while my breasts were in the mouth of my Son, I used to see angels and heavenly beings standing before us, genuflecting and worshiping at the holy feet of my Son while crying out and saying: "Blessed are you, O God, who chose this humility for the salvation of Adam and his children whom you have fashioned with your hands! Blessed be the first Word that came out of the mouth of the Father, the Lord of all! Honor is due to your virgin mother who endured pain with you at your holy birth!" At the end of all this we sat and rested from the weariness that overtook us and the angels used to come constantly and comfort us.

After this Satan appeared to Herod[43], spoke to him and said to him: "What gain was it to you? You slew the innocent children of Bethlehem in order to find Mary and her Son, and you did not find them. I shall tell you where and in what locality they are: the woman and her Son are hidden in a desert place of the southern side of the land of Egypt. They live in a forsaken house in which there is no other besides themselves, in the direction which I mentioned to you. Arise and dispatch ten soldiers of yours to repair to that place and kill them, and you will be confirmed in your kingdom. If you do not listen to me and do what I am telling you, tomorrow this child will grow up and go to Jerusalem, He and His mother, and He will perform numerous and great miracles. The children of Israel will then reject the idols, whose cult will cease. He will also put to shame the priests and the heads of the people, will take your Kingdom from you and will dominate all the people. Lo, I have told you what will happen to you. When your soldiers depart to inquire after them, let them proceed as far as the town known as Ḳuskam and then let them travel to the west side of it as far as the mountain, until they have found them in the place where they are living alone[44], because they have scoured all the land of Egypt and have not found anybody who would give them hospitality."

When Satan finished his story he disappeared, and Herod became incensed with rage, and he assembled all the chiefs and elders, and spoke to them and narrated to them what had taken place. And they answered and said: "O our lord, let it be as you wish." And their anger against my beloved Son persisted till they crucified Him. And Herod made inquiries concerning the majority of the soldiers and selected ten valiant men from amongst them and gave them information about the place in which we were bound to be found, and he said to them: "When you shall have found them bring them to me in order that I may kill them with my own hands. If you do what I have ordered you I will give each one of you ten talents of gold, and you will be great in all my kingdom." When they heard these words from the king they left him in haste and went to do what he had ordered them, and then take the gold which he had promised to them. And they mounted their steeds in order to pursue us.

And there was a man from the children of Israel, of the tribe of Judah and of the family of the Kings, who was related to Joseph. He was from his

---

[43] Herod, even at the apex of his political power has not remote jurisdiction in Upper Egypt. Moreover, he is unable to do much to extradite anyone from another sovereign power, as Egypt is under the direct authority of Caesar Augustus.

[44] This is a significant geography location to the Coptic faith, it is known as Deir el-Muharraq, and maintains a monastery on this site. By Egyptian church tradition it is the oldest church in the land of Egypt, being built personally by St. Mark the Evangelist upon his arrival in the country.

childhood a valiant man and a giant and was called Moses[45]. When he heard this news he said to himself: "I shall rise and go to Joseph His father and apprise him of what took place. I shall also take them out of the place in which they are from fear lest these cruel men should discover their whereabouts and kill them. I shall tell them that I have arrived before these men by the power and help of God."

And God granted him great speed and Divine power, and he came to us in three days, because he traveled in the night more than in the day. He made inquiries and went to all the places in which we had walked, until he reached this mountain in which we are. And Satan met him in this desert and said to him: "O Moses, where are you going alone in this desert?" And Moses narrated to him all that had taken place. And Satan answered like a frightened man and said to him: "O Moses, you toiled and labored in vain because lo the soldiers are preceding you and are hastening before you. If you will listen to me do not go further and toil and exhaust yourself in vain." And Moses answered the demon: "Allow me to go now to my country lest the troops of whom you spoke should come and see me here and kill me; I have nothing left now but to return to my house." Moses said all this with the intention of laughing at the demon and making fun of him. And after Satan had heard these things from Moses he disappeared from his sight.

And Moses directed his course to us in fear, and he came to us in the morning while Salome was bathing my Son in this house. When the old Joseph saw him he recognized him and rose up to greet him. And Moses answered and said to Joseph: "What are you doing in this locality in ignorance of what took place in these regions and of what Herod did and how he killed the children of Bethlehem and Jerusalem and how he searched for this child and did not find Him? It has been revealed to him by the demon that you were in this mountain, and thereupon he has dispatched ten of his soldiers to come and kill you here, and lo they have arrived in this locality a long time ago. When I heard this, I came to you in order to acquaint you with the facts."

When I heard this my knees shook, and I took my Son from Salome and climbed to the upper chamber which had windows. I sat in the northern window which looks upon the road and I wailed and said: "Woe is me, O my

---

[45] This reference to a member of the Davidic family abiding in Egypt is intriguing. It is possible that it is only allegorical, as the name Moses was not in common use at the time. Nonetheless, the sojourn deep into the heart of Egypt would make more sense if there were family members who could offer the family asylum. Moreover, Joseph's connection with Egypt would explain the oddity of his alleged brother Cleophas' name, as well as the absence of nativity stories about Joseph the Carpenter in the early church.

beloved Son! If they came and killed, you the fatigue which I have endured with you down to this day will have been in vain. Woe is me, O my beloved Son, because the one who brought this intelligence to me to-day resembles the messenger who came to Job in his time and said to him: 'Your ten sons have died.' Woe is me, O my beloved Son, because fear has taken possession of me, and I have no strength to rise up! Woe is me, O my beloved Son, because of this evil news which has reached me!

"Woe is me, O light of my eyes! What shall I do when I see the soldiers of the wicked Herod coming here and snatching you from my hands? What shall I do, O my beloved Son, when I see you in their hands, and they will not let me come near you? Woe is me, O my beloved Son! If I had known this before I would have fled to dry mountains from these persecutors so that perchance I might have been saved. I have left my country and all other countries and have come to this place. O my beloved Son, lift up your eyes and look at your lonely and wretched mother, and see the anguish that is in my heart. I have no power of thought, and lo I became to-day like the other women whose sons have been killed by Herod.

"O my Son! Let sun, moon and stars weep with me today. Let them weep over my wretchedness and exile. I implore the prophet David to come and weep with me because I have looked for someone to lament with me and have not found any. I pray my Father Jacob, who wept over Joseph, to come and witness my anguish and the sadness of my heart, because my Son is an only child, and I have no other one besides Him, and cruel men wish to kill Him. I implore Jeremiah today to come, wail, lament and weep with me because I am in a strange country and I do not know what to do. I have no knowledge of any town or any village. Would to God they had left me alone in this loneliness! The tears that are in my eyes have dried up and I do not know what to do."

While I was lamenting in this way and contemplating the pure body of my Son, He said to me: "O my holy mother, receive power from me and be not afraid. You have wept and lamented enough, for your weeping, your lamentation and your wailing have reached my heart. May the will of my Father be done! Let us go down to the old Joseph and to Salome and see what we ought to do." When He uttered to me these words my heart was strengthened and we came down; and He spoke to old Joseph and said: "O father, be of good cheer." And He turned to the man whose name was Moses and said to him: "You came to us in order to inform us. Your coming and your trouble will be rewarded, but because of the fear which has been caused to you by my mother, take hold of this stone on which I was bathed and put it under your head, sleep, and rest a short while, and I shall place your soul with Abraham, Isaac and Jacob until I have delivered Adam and his posterity;

and then I shall bring you to my Kingdom." And he took the stone and placed it under his head and turning his head towards the east he gave up the ghost. Then old Joseph buried his body and interred it in this house under the threshold towards the interior. And his memory survives down to this day.

After this we lived several days in this house, until we completed six months in it. The first day we came to it was the sixth of Barmūdah[46] and the day we left it was the sixth of Babah[47]. And the number of all the days which we spent in it while we were fleeing from the accursed Herod–from the day in which we went out of Bethlehem and came to this mountain of Ḳuskam to the day in which we returned to our town which is Nazareth–is three years and six months.

While the old Joseph was asleep, lo the angel of the Lord appeared to him in a dream and said to him: "O Joseph, son of David, arise and take the Child and His mother, because Herod has died a grievous and painful death. Arise thou and go into the land of Israel. The soldiers which he had dispatched after the Child have all died on the way and gone to hell. Be not afraid, the Lord is with you."

In the morning Joseph narrated to us what he had seen in his night dream, and we were greatly pleased and we prepared to set out. And I spoke to my beloved Son and said to Him: "I beseech you, O my beloved Son, to grant honor and esteem to this house which gave us shelter in our exile and in which we lived." And He opened His holy mouth and blessed the house and said: "Let the benediction of My good Father remain in this house for ever. This house which you see, O my holy mother, will have in it a sanctuary dedicated to God, and people will offer sacrifices and ex-votos in it to the Lord, and those who will offer them will be the faithful of the orthodox faith till the day of my second coming. It will have a lamp which will burn in the middle of it forever.

"All those who come to this house with faith and worship and pray therein shall be blessed, and I will forgive all their sins, if they intend not to revert to them, and I will count them among the saints. If any of those who are in distress, trouble or loss come to this holy place and worship and pray in it, and demand congruous things, I will grant their requests and all their demands.

"If the one who comes be a husbandman, I will bless his crops, and if he be a shepherd I will bless his flocks, and if he be a clerk, I will bless his pen. If any

---

[46] The Coptic month of Parmouti, which is March 31st.
[47] The Coptic month of Paopi, which is October 16th.

of those who are versed in any craft come and pray in this house, I will bless their craft. If any of those who are affected with a disease of any kind whatsoever come and pray in this holy house, I will heal all their bodies. If any of those who are in trouble or anguish on account of children who have died, or on account of beasts or of robbers or of kings, remember this holy house in which we are, and pray to me and to my good and compassionate Father who is in Heaven, I will deliver them from all their trials and troubles.

"O Mary, my mother, this house in which we are will contain holy monks on whom no ruler of the world shall be able to inflict any injury, because it became a refuge to us. And any barren woman who beseeches me with a pure heart and remembers this house, I will give her sons. All the people who came to this place with ex-votos and offerings for your holy name, I will inscribe my name on their offerings and on their sacrifices as it happened to Abel in his days when he offered a sacrifice before me. I have anathematized this town which did not receive us in our exile and blessed all the villages that surround it. Let my blessing and my protection be on their inhabitants, on their children, on their property, on their land and all that which they possess. Let no one who hates my name ever inhabit them, because you dwelt in this place.

"There will be in this place a blessed congregation who will remember and bless my name, and pray to me at all times, and so gain strength against all their adversaries. As to this house nothing shall be demolished from it nor shall anything be added to it. I tell you now that if any chief or ruler should from this time inflict any harm on it, I will put him to shame and confusion for all time, because I inhabited it and the angels provided for us in it, since I did not find any earthly food in it.

"I will place in it my blessing and the protection of my Father for ever and ever. Anyone who comes to this place and honors my name and your name, his house will be full of all good things. Those women in travail who will remember me and remember the fatigue that you endured with me, I will hear their prayers and they shall be relieved. O my holy virgin mother, there will be sanctuaries built under your name and my name in those places in which you have halted. And my blessing and the protection of my Father will dwell in this house for ever and ever, Amen." And we said: "Amen."

After my Son had spoken, thus we rose up and descended from the mountain. We reached the town of Eshmunain and its inhabitants received us with great joy and jubilation. When morning came, I carried my Son on my arms, and we came to the sea, where we looked for a ship but found none ready. Then my beloved Son made the sign of the Cross on the water, and it became like a ship before us[48]. We then went onboard, and we arrived at Nazareth and gave thanks to God[49]. He appeared also several times after His ascent to Heaven.

One day I was in the house of Mary, mother of John, who was afterwards called Mark the Evangelist. It is he who came to the land of Egypt, the inhabitants of which believed through him, when he announced to them the Kingdom of God. It is the one whose inheritance and office you took, O Theophilus. The Apostles were also there, and they alluded to the wickedness done by Judas to my beloved Son, the true Son of God. And I answered and said to them while weeping bitterly: "O my brethren and beloved of my Son, I testify to you that from the day of my annunciation by the angel Gabriel down to this hour, I have wept because of the cruel thing that the Jews did to me and to my Son when they slapped my face on account of my conception and the birth of my Child."

And Peter answered and said to me: "O Lady of all of us, we implore you to reveal to us your trials, so that we may hear them, and so that when we go and preach the Kingdom of Heaven to mankind, we may remember you and narrate all that happened to you." And I began to narrate to them what happened to be from the day I went to Elizabeth, and how my Son was born in a place while I was alone, and what happened in my journey to the land of Egypt, and my coming to this desert place, and the injustice done to us by the accursed Herod. When I narrated this while weeping to all the Apostles, there were present with me Mary Magdalene, Hannah, and Salome.

In that hour my Lord and my Son revealed Himself to me in a sitting posture, while the Seraphim, Gabriel and Michael and innumerable angels were glorifying Him. And He stood in the middle and said to us: "Peace be with all of you." And we rose up immediately and worshiped at His feet. And my Son

---

[48] The Coptic Synaxarion notes that the family left Egypt in the same way that they came. If this is true, then their arrival in Egypt would have been procured by boat, which would explain why no villages in Lower Egypt are mentioned. There is an additional Coptic legend which associates the church in Old Cairo, the ancient Church of St. Sergius with a port used by the family of Christ. This is perhaps a historically responsible site for a Jewish political exile to choose, as it already contained an Egyptian Jewish community. Moreover, it was unaffiliated with the political nature of the Jewish community at Leontopolis, or the much larger and Hellenic community in Alexandria. There are also surviving oral traditions in the Coptic church that members of Joseph's family were residing there, and gave them hospitality while they were in Egypt.

[49] This is geographically impossible, as Nazareth in a hillside village in the Galilee, not a Mediterranean port. Navel passage is possible, but the port of arrival would likely have been Caesarea. It does appear that the author of this text has limited knowledge of the geography of the Levant, or the regions outside of Lower Egypt.

turned to me and said to me: "O my holy virgin mother, why are you in tears and anguish? Lo I have prepared for you in heaven joy and gladness which have no end. Do not weep and lament because of (my) death; you should rather rejoice at my resurrection from the dead because I have saved the world–you who walked with me in foreign countries and in a forsaken desert, as far as this forsaken place which I will bless with my holy hands before any other Church is dedicated to my name."

In that hour He commanded a luminous cloud which came down and carried us all and placed us in this holy house, O Theophilus, and it was the third hour of the day, which was the sixth of the month of Hatūr, which corresponds with the second day of October.

When the Apostles were ready for the consecration of the Church, Gabriel and Michael carried the vessel containing the water which my beloved Son sprinkled on the Church. I and the twelve Apostles were present at the consecration of this house; and Mary Magdalene and Salome were also present; and there was no church built in the world before it. And this Church was consecrated by our Savior Jesus Christ before the Apostles went out to preach the Gospel of the Kingdom of God. At the time of the consecration, He uttered the following words: "The hands that have fashioned you, O Adam, have consecrated this house, and the hands in which nails have been driven on the Golgotha, have blessed this house. Amen. Amen." And we all answered and said: "Amen."

Afterwards we found vestments ready along with the ritual used by the Church. When everything was ready, He ordered Peter to celebrate the Mass, and then the Holy Spirit came down. He then commanded the Apostles to remember their parents who had passed away, and He ordered also in that hour the souls of their parents who had departed to come and enter the sanctuary; and they came at that moment in the form in which they were with us in the flesh, and He baptized them with the water that had remained from the consecration of the Church; and He gave His holy Body and ordered them to say the Mass and to remember at the moment of the offering of the sacrifice upon the holy altars their parents who had passed away. And our Lord fortified them, comforted them, and gave them peace.

In that very moment a large bird flew from heaven and came down carrying with it all good things in matter of wines and delicacies. And it came down in the center of the Church and we took from it what we wanted.

The angels stood then above our heads like deacons, and the apostles were joyful and glad because they had seen their parents and because of the glory and majesty of that hour. And our Savior spoke with them and said to them:

"Let this day be a remembrance to you forever. And I will command that a church be built under your name on this mountain." And the Apostles answered and said to Him: "Glory be to you; and honor, worship, power and omnipotence belong to you because you have exalted us above all the creation." And a cloud took us again and placed us at sunset in the house in which we were previously in Jerusalem. We came back to Jerusalem on the same day we had left it.

This is what you asked me to tell you, O Theophilus. I told you all at this moment. Tell to all the world what I have narrated to you and what has happened to us, and write it down to us as a memorial for ever and ever. Arise now and offer sacrifice for the monks and for all the people who have congregated here to-day, because I will bless them before I go, as this day is the day of my Commemoration and of my leaving of the body. As to you be of good cheer because in your remaining days no harm and no anguish will befall you, and no evil of any kind will affect this church in your time."

This story was told to me, and these words were uttered to me Theophilus the servant of Christ and your servant, O my brethren and my beloved. I have narrated to-day to your love what the holy Virgin Mary mother of God narrated to me, O you all who believe in Christ. God knows that I have not added anything to, nor taken away anything from what our Lady Mary, mother of God, said to me, and what I heard from her. As to you, listen to it, believe in it, and let your heart not be in doubt.

And I Theophilus answered and said to our Lady: "Blessed are you among women, O our Lady Mary, mother of God. We came to-day and rejoiced at the sweetness of your words which are like honeycomb and like the wine that maketh glad the heart of man." We have acknowledged the honor and glory of this holy house from the fact that the Lord of this world and His holy virgin mother dwelt in it.

O my beloved, none of those who intend to go back to their sins should enter this holy house, because our Lord Jesus Christ and His holy virgin mother dwelt in it, and because all the hierarchies of the holy angels observe this day as a feast in purity and holiness. No thief and no one who is under the influence of sin should enter this house, because Paul says: "Neither those who commit sins, nor the fornicators, nor the publicans, nor the idolators, nor those who perpetuate other crimes shall inherit the Kingdom of God." We ought also to remember that we shall leave our bodies and go to God our Lord, and that we shall rise again in that place of truth, where we shall answer for all that we have done whether it be good or bad.

We should also refrain our souls from theft, our bodies from fornication, and our eyes from evil sights, diabolical passion and covetousness. We should also refrain our tongues from all bad and impure curses, from oath and from all evil things which bring no honor but dishonor. We should also refrain our soul from hatred and false witness. Let us extirpate from our hearts these and similar things, because it is they that lead men to hell, the fire of which is not quenched. Let us purify our bodies from sin and then partake of the body of our Lord Jesus Christ for the forgiveness of our sins and be worthy of the blessings of our holy Lady Mary, the mother of God, and observe her feast to-day.

What good can a fornicator derive and gain can accrue to him if he comes to the holy Mary, the mother of the King of Kings, and enters her holy house, while he does not repent of his iniquity? And what utility can an adulteress derive from entering this holy house in order to be worthy of the one who brought forth the Christ, unless she confesses her sins? She will then pray and implore her Son and her Lord on our behalf, because she is full of mercy. We ought also to carry our offerings and bring our ex-votos with a pure heart, and then stretch our hands to her holy Son and ask for His body and His innocent blood.

Blessed be he who comes to this house, because he will meet with good things in this world, and when he leaves this earthly body, he will go to the Kingdom of Heaven! Woe to the one who commits a sin in this house because God will be angry with him as He was with Herod. Blessed be he who hears and believes and does not entertain any doubt concerning you, O our Lord Jesus Christ! Blessed be the one who sees this holy house, because the Lord will place him in the bosom of our father Abraham and will answer his prayers in this world through the good works that he will do! Woe to the one who vows something to this house and refuses to acknowledge his vow and does no fulfill it. The Holy Spirit will be far from such a one.

Were it not that I see the greatness of the number of the people assembled here and their joy on the occasion of this high feast, I would have told many more miracles in order to exalt this holy house. This house is the beginning of the forgiveness of sins. This house is all of it benediction, and anyone who enters into it shall be blessed by God and by His mother, the holy Virgin. This house is the tryst of the Lord, of His angels, of His Apostles, and of the heavenly hierarchies, and were it not for the fact that I am entrusted with the care of the diocese and the congregation of Orthodoxy, I would not have left this place, till the day of my death; God, however, will count to me what I had intended to do.

May God bless the young and the old among you, and may He grant to you the good reward of your labors in coming to this place from far and near! May He bless your fields and hold your believing kings in His keeping! May He lay your enemies under your feet, and sow peace and concord in the churches and in the monasteries all the days of your life, in order that you may observe this day with joy and partake of the body and blood of our Lord Jesus Christ! May He forgive your old sins and place His fear in your hearts, in order that you may be consecrated to-day to Him! May you be in His keeping in order that you may reach your homes in the peace of God! Amen.

May He grant the blessings of this holy house to you and to anyone who sets foot in this place, which is the place in which dwelt our Lord Jesus Christ and His holy mother! And as He granted you to assemble and congregate in this holy house, He is able to make you worthy of assembling together in His Kingdom with His saints.

And I, Cyril, was with my Father, the Patriarch Theophilus, and heard from his holy mouth this story which I have written down.

When the people heard this discourse, they rejoiced greatly and raised their voices and glorified God with a high and loud voice.

Glory be to the Holy Trinity, Father, Son and Holy Spirit, now, always and for ever and ever. Amen.

Here ends the third book containing the vision of the Holy Theophilus, Patriarch of Alexandria. May his prayer be with us. Amen.

www.ingramcontent.com/pod-product-compliance
Lightning Source LLC
Chambersburg PA
CBHW051601120626
46551CB00013B/1625